All About
WILD
WEATHER

Amazing climates that change our world

Robin Kerrod

CONSULTANT Helen Young, BBC Weather Centre

southwater

This edition is published by Southwater

Southwater is an imprint of Anness Publishing Ltd
Hermes House, 88–89 Blackfriars Road, London SE1 8HA
tel. 020 7401 2077; fax 020 7633 9499
www.southwaterbooks.com; info@anness.com

UK agent: The Manning Partnership Ltd,
6 The Old Dairy, Melcombe Road, Bath BA2 3LR;
tel. 01225 478444; fax 01225 478440; sales@manning-partnership.co.uk

UK distributor: Grantham Book Services Ltd,
Isaac Newton Way, Alma Park Industrial Estate, Grantham, Lincs NG31 9SD;
tel. 01476 541080; fax 01476 541061; orders@gbs.tbs-ltd.co.uk

North American agent/distributor: National Book Network,
4501 Forbes Boulevard, Suite 200, Lanham, MD 20706;
tel. 301 459 3366; fax 301 429 5746; www.nbnbooks.com

Australian agent/distributor: Pan Macmillan Australia,
Level 18, St Martins Tower, 31 Market St, Sydney, NSW 2000;
tel. 1300 135 113; fax 1300 135 103; customer.service@macmillan.com.au

New Zealand agent/distributor: David Bateman Ltd,
30 Tarndale Grove, Off Bush Road, Albany, Auckland;
tel. (09) 415 7664; fax (09) 415 8892

A CIP catalogue record for this book is available from the British Library.

Publisher: Joanna Lorenz
Managing Editor, Children's Books: Gilly Cameron Cooper
Senior Editor: Lisa Miles
Editor: Leon Gray
Consultant: Helen Young
Designer: Caroline Reeves
Photographer: John Freeman
Stylist: Thomasina Smith
Picture Researchers: Liz Eddison, Susannah Parker, Gwen Campbell
Illustrators: Peter Bull Art Studio, Guy Smith
Production Controller: Claire Rae

Previously published as *Investigations Wild Weather*

10 9 8 7 6 5 4 3 2 1

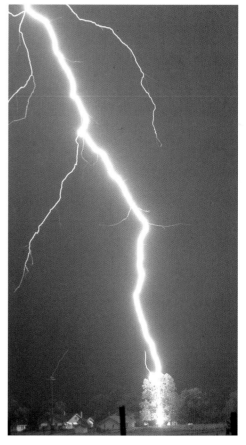

PICTURE CREDITS

b= bottom, t= top, c= centre, l= left, r= right
The Ancient Art & Architecture Collection: 32c. The Art Archive: 6tl. BBC Natural History Unit: /Doug Wechsler: 15cl. Bruce Coleman:
10bl, 54cl; /Michael Freeman: 45br; /Tore Hagman: 39cl; /Johnny Johnson: cover br, 55tr; / Dr Scott Nielsen: 38br, 39tl & 39br; /Mary
Plage: 41br; /John Shaw: 13bl; /Kim Taylor: 40cr. Getty One Stone: 5bl, 7bl, 12tl, 16bl, 18c, 23cl, 52tr, 53cl, 54br, 58bl; /Glen Allison: 16cr;
/David Austen: 11br; /John Beatty: 49cl; /Peter Cade: 23tr; /J F Causse: 19br; /Chris Cheadle: 17d & 46tr; /Darrell Gulin: 35b; /Paul
Kenward: 18tl; /Laurence Dutton: 57br; /David Hiser: 55bl; /Jerry Kobalenko: 26bl; /Hiroyuki Matsumoto: 7tr; /Alan Moller: 5br & 27tr;
/Ian Murphy: 42tr; /Frank Oberle: 5tr; /Martin Puddy: 48tl; /James Randklev: 35cr; /Peter Rauter: cover c, 26br, 63; /Jurgen Reisch: 16tr;
/Lorne Resnick: 17bl, 62; /Manoj Shah: 49tl; /Robin Smith: 7br; /Brian Stablyk: 17br; /Bill Staley: 40cl; /Vince Streano: 15tr; /Michael
Townsend: 55tl; /Larry Ulrich: back cover bc, 5tl; /John Warden: 35tl; /Art Wolfe: 17tr; /Darrel Wong: 19tl. Mary Evans Picture Library: 44tl,
56bl; /A Rackham: 53tr. Geoscience Features Library: 34tl. Hulton Getty: 22cr& 28c. National Meteorological Library: 59tl. NHPA: /B&C
Alexander: 55br. Panos Pictures: 15b, 15cr, 31cr, 41cn, 48br, 49br & 49cr. Powerstock Zefa: 4br, 26tl, 31bl, 33br & 44bl. Rex Features: 53b;
/Pascal Fayolle: 52cr. Robert Harding: endpapers, cover c. Robin Kerrod: 8br, 19tr, 23cr, 36tl, 40bl, 41cl, 42cr, 53tl & 54tl. Science Photo
Library: cover tr, 3cr, 3tr, 14tr, 30tr, 31tl, 38tr, 44tr, 48bl, 59tr, 59br, 59bl; /Johnny Autrey: 2, 45l; /Alex Bartel: 56br; /Tony Craddock: 3tl,
35cl; /Gregory Dinijan: 10br; /Margaret Durrance: 27c ; /Graham Ewens: 27bl; /Simon Fraser: 9bl; /Jim Goodwin: back cover l/John
Howard: 51b; /Phil Jude: back cover br; 37bl; /Keith Kent: 39bl; /Peter Menzel: 59c; /NASA: 31br; /Donna & Stephen O'Meara: 57tl;
/David Parker: 42bl, 45tr & 58br; /Pekka Parviainen: 32tr; /Francoise Sauze: 28tr; /A C Twomey: 3 bl, 52bl. Spacecharts: 18bl, 57tr & 58tl.
Stockmarket: 30b. Trip: 8bl & 60tl.

Every effort has been made to trace the copyright holders of all images that appear in this book. Anness Publishing Ltd apologises for any
unintentional omissions and, if notified, would be happy to add an acknowledgement in future editions.

The publishers would like to thank the following children for modelling in this book:
Maria Bloodworth, Tony Borg, Steven Briggs, Jackie Ishiekwene, Daniel Johnson, Jon Leaning, Erin Macarthy, Hanife Manur, Tanya Martin,
Lola Olayinka, Ini Usoro. Additional thanks to Caroline Beattie and to West Meters Ltd for the loan of props.

WILD WEATHER

CONTENTS

4	What is weather?	34	The water cycle
6	Heat from the sun	36	Humidity
8	Measuring temperature	38	Looking at clouds
10	Climates of the world	40	Rain and dew
12	Changing the temperature	42	Making rainbows
14	El Niño and La Niña	44	Thunder and lightning
16	Beating the heat	46	Charging up
18	Where the weather is	48	Flood and drought
20	In the air	50	Gauging the rain
22	Air on the move	52	Snow and ice
24	Air pressure	54	Coping with cold
26	Whirlwinds and tornadoes	56	Ice age or greenhouse?
28	Measuring the wind	58	Studying the weather
30	Hurricanes and cyclones	60	Your weather station
32	Masses of air	62	Glossary
		64	Index

WHAT IS WEATHER?

Some of the greatest challenges humans face are environmental disasters caused by the weather—from droughts and famines to blizzards and flash floods. Dealing with these conditions is an inevitable part of life on our planet. Sometimes the weather only affects our lives in a small way, such as in choosing what clothes to wear or where to go on vacation. At other times, its consequences can be much more serious, as those who have seen the power of a tornado can testify.

Since the weather influences our lives in so many ways, scientists called meteorologists study patterns in the weather and try to forecast, or predict, what it is going to be like in the future. As research and technology advance, these predictions have become increasingly accurate.

Sense in the sun
Many people find long, hot summer days a pleasant time of year, but the sun can burn your skin if you do not protect it. You should use sunscreen but, also always keep your skin covered up. Wear a sun hat to protect your head and sunglasses to cover your eyes.

Dress up warm
Waterproof clothes, an umbrella and boots will protect you from the bad weather in most countries. But some places, such as the Arctic, are so cold that exposure to the icy temperatures there may be life-threatening.

Snow fun
Many people enjoy playing in the snow during the winter. But a heavy snowfall accompanied by a strong wind causes blizzard conditions, which make the outdoors a very dangerous place to be.

Dry as dust
Death Valley in California is one of the hottest places in the world. Rain sometimes falls and collects in small pools. But the water soon evaporates, leaving the cracked ground seen here.

Water everywhere
Heavy rain has caused flooding in the town of Kaskakia in Illinois. Local rivers have burst their banks, and many people's homes have been submerged.

Winding up
A satellite picture reveals a tropical storm developing in the middle of the Pacific Ocean. Clouds spiral around the center of an area of low pressure, driven by winds that may reach speeds of up to 120mph.

Terror twister
A tornado powers its way through a small town in Texas. The rapidly swirling winds of a tornado, or twister, can devastate buildings, uproot trees and toss vehicles into the air, cutting a path of destruction.

HEAT FROM THE SUN

THE sun is a gigantic star that pours out vast amounts of energy, called electromagnetic radiation, into space. Although just a tiny amount of this energy reaches Earth, it is enough to make rocks so hot that eggs can be fried on them. This heat energy also stirs the atmosphere into motion, powering Earth's different weather systems.

Different parts of Earth receive different amounts of heat from the sun. The lower the sun is in the sky, the less heat it provides. The sun is directly overhead at the equator, so it is much warmer there than at the earth's poles. Some of the sun's energy is reflected by the earth's clouds, some by the ground and some by the atmosphere. The amount of heat that any one place receives from the sun also changes from season to season.

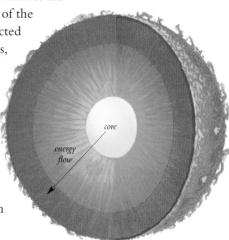

Sun worship
An ancient Egyptian relief carved from limestone shows the pharaoh Akhenaten. He is offering sacred lotus flowers to the sun god, Aten. The ancient Egyptian people worshipped the sun god because they recognized that life depended on the sun. They kept track of time by watching the sun rise and fall in the sky, and they realized that their crops depended on the sun to survive.

Hot stuff
The sun's energy is produced in its center, called the core, where the temperature reaches 27,000,000°F. At this temperature, gases fuse (combine) to produce vast amounts of energy in the form of electromagnetic radiation, most of which is released as heat and light.

Heating Earth
The sun pours energy onto earth as heat and light. Some bounces off a thin blanket of gases, known as the atmosphere, back into space. The rest heats up the oceans, land and air. At night, clouds in the atmosphere help stop heat from escaping back into space.

energy produced by the sun

energy reflected back into space

energy absorbed by the oceans

energy absorbed by the land

Snowy December

During the winter in New York City,, it often snows in December and is bitterly cold. The temperature may be just above the freezing point (32°F), and a biting cold wind will make it feel even colder. New York is in the Northern Hemisphere. In this part of the world, the coldest part of winter begins in December. This is the time of year when the Northern Hemisphere is tilted most away from the sun.

March

Earth's orbit

December

June

sun

September

The changing seasons

Any one place on Earth does not always receive the same amount of energy from the sun. In fact, it changes with the seasons. The most energy is received in the summer season and the least in the winter season. The seasons change because Earth's axis is tilted in space. In summer, one half, or hemisphere, tilts toward the sun and is warmer. In winter, the hemisphere tilts away from the sun, and it is colder here.

Harnessing the sun

A huge solar power plant in California converts energy from the sun into electrical energy. Giant mirrors reflect sunlight onto a tank of water at the top of the tower. The water gets hot and boils, creating steam, which drives giant turbines that generate the electricity. Solar power plants are useful in warm climates where the sun shines steadily most of the time.

Sunny December

In December, temperatures can exceed 86°F on beaches in Australia. Australia is in the Southern Hemisphere, where seasons are opposite from those in the Northern Hemisphere.

MEASURING TEMPERATURE

WHAT we notice most about the weather is the temperature—that is, how hot or cold it is. Temperature is measured using a thermometer. There are many different types of thermometer, but the most common consists of a glass column partially filled with a liquid such as alcohol or mercury (a liquid metal). When the temperature increases, the liquid expands in proportion to the rise in temperature and increases in length up the glass column. Similarly, a decrease in temperature causes the liquid in the glass column to decrease in length. This means that thermometers can record a range of temperatures. The simple thermometer in the experiment is made using water and can be used to record changes in temperature.

A simple thermometer
The temperature of the air can be measured using a simple mercury thermometer. Most have two temperature scales: degrees Celsius (°C) and degrees Fahrenheit (°F).

FACT BOX

• The human body is normally a constant temperature of 98.6°F.

• In 1922, the air temperature in Al´Aziziyah, Libya, rose to a sweltering 136°F in the shade.

• Water freezes into solid ice when the temperature falls below 0°C.

• Some parts of the Northern Hemisphere experience winter temperatures that regularly fall below −58°F.

• At a temperature of −310°F, all the air present in our atmosphere would turn into a liquid.

• When low temperatures combine with strong winds, our surroundings feel a lot colder than the temperature alone would suggest. This effect is known as the "wind-chill factor." For example, a combination of a wind speed of 30mph and a temperature of just 39°F produces a wind-chill factor of 12°F, although water will not freeze in these conditions.

Taking your temperature
A thin strip of heat-sensitive material, called a thermo-strip, can be used to record the temperature of the human body. If you press the thermo-strip against your forehead, the heat of your body makes the strip change color. The body temperature of a healthy human should be about 98.6°F.

Highs and lows
A maximum-and-minimum thermometer is used to check a range of temperatures inside a greenhouse. This type of thermometer indicates the highest and lowest temperature in 24 hours. If the temperature drops below 32°F, the girl's tomato plant will die.

MAKE YOUR OWN THERMOMETER

You will need: cold water, plastic bottle, food coloring, straw, reusable adhesive, piece of card stock, scissors, felt-tip pen

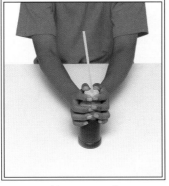

1 Pour cold water into the empty bottle until it is about two-thirds full. Add some food coloring. Dip the straw into the water and seal the neck tightly with reusable adhesive.

2 Blow into the straw to force extra air into the bottle. After a few seconds, the extra air pressure inside the bottle will force the water to move up inside the straw.

3 Cut two slots on either side of the card stock. Slide it over the straw. Let the bottle stand. Mark the card next to the water level to record the temperature of the room.

4 Then take your thermometer outside and let stand for a while. On a hot day, the heat from the sun will gradually make the air and water in the bottle expand. This will force water up the straw and past the level you marked for the room temperature. Mark the card stock again to show the temperature outside. Now put your thermometer in the refrigerator for two hours. The water level in the tube will drop below the room temperature mark. Make a note on your thermometer.

Stevenson screen
A meteorologist notes the temperature recorded by a pair of thermometers housed inside a shelter called a Stevenson screen. This protects the instruments from the weather. It is painted white to reflect sunlight and has louvered (slatted) sides to keep the air inside the shelter at the same temperature as the air outside.

CLIMATES OF THE WORLD

DIFFERENT parts of the world receive different amounts of heat from the sun. As a result, they have a particular weather pattern throughout the year. This changing pattern is called the climate. The world can be divided into regions with similar climates that suit different kinds of animals and plants.

In some regions near the equator, the climate is hot all year round, and plenty of rain also falls. Vast areas of tree-covered land, called rainforests, flourish there because of the heavy rainfall. On either side of the equator, hot grasslands, called savannas, experience rain for only part of the year. Hot deserts are also found in this part of the world. Hardly any rain falls in deserts. Farther north and south, the climate is neither too hot nor too cold, and rain regularly falls. This is a warm temperate climate, common to most parts of the United States and Europe. However, the northernmost parts of North America, Europe and Asia have a cold temperate climate. The winters are long and cold, and plenty of snow falls. Evergreen forests dominate the landscape. In the far north of North America, Europe and Asia, it is too cold for trees to grow. These regions are called the tundra, and the temperatures may fall to −75°F. At the other end of Earth, the continent of Antarctica has an equally cold climate.

Key to the climate
A world map can be divided into zones corresponding to the different types of weather patterns throughout the year. These are called climatic zones. Scientists classify climates in many different ways. The climate map below is divided into six different kinds of climate. Regions with different climates are inhabited by different types of animals and plants, which are well adapted to survive in their particular environments.

KEY

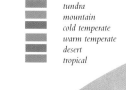

tundra
mountain
cold temperate
warm temperate
desert
tropical

Grazing the tundra
Caribou graze the thin vegetation of the Arctic tundra. The tundra has a harsh climate. In the winter it is extremely cold, and it only improves moderately in the summer. Most parts of the tundra are snowswept and frozen for up to nine months of the year.

In the tropics
Regions near the equator have a tropical climate, which means it is very wet and warm. These conditions are ideal for rapid plant growth, creating rainforests. The trees and shrubs are evergreens, which means they keep their leaves all year long.

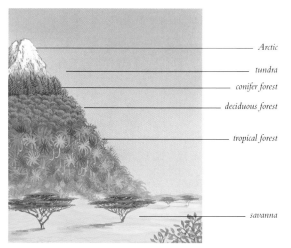

Arctic
tundra
conifer forest
deciduous forest
tropical forest
savanna

Mountain zones

Generally, the climate of a place is decided by its position on earth, but its altitude, or height above sea level, is also important. The temperature falls as you climb above sea level. Mountains in most parts of the world are layered with many zones, which have particular types of vegetation. These correspond with the climatic zones around the world.

Different types of mountains have different zonation. Generally, the Arctic zone is at the top, followed by tundra, then coniferous forest (evergreen trees with needle-shaped leaves), then deciduous forest (where the trees lose their leaves in winter). As the climate warms at lower levels, the vegetation becomes tropical forest, and finally savanna at the bottom.

An imaginary line called the snow line divides the Arctic and tundra zones. Above this line, there is a year-round cover of snow. Another imaginary line, called the tree line, divides the tundra and coniferous forest zones. Above this line, trees do not grow.

Desert rock
A desert region surrounds Ayers Rock, or Uluru, which is an immense sandstone rock in the middle of the Outback in Australia. The scrubby plants around Ayers Rock flower after the brief but heavy rains that occasionally fall.

CHANGING THE TEMPERATURE

Cool color
In hot places, such as this town in Spain, all the houses are whitewashed to reflect the sunlight and keep the people inside cool. There is not a dark house to be seen, because dark houses warm up faster by day and cool down faster at night.

DARK AND LIGHT

You will need: *two identical glass jars with lids (paint the outside of one black and the other white), sand, watch, thermometer, notebook, pen*

T HE TEMPERATURE of a place is controlled by different factors. The main factor is the amount of energy a place absorbs from the sun, but other conditions play a part in controlling temperature, too. For instance, areas at very high altitudes are much colder than areas at sea level. Another factor is distance of a place from the sea. This is because the continents and the oceans do not heat up and cool down in the same way as each other. Water takes longer to heat up than the land, but the water holds its heat for much longer. Therefore, summers are cooler and winters are milder on the coast than they are inland.

Since water can circulate, it can move the heat from place to place in the form of ocean currents. Ocean currents therefore often affect air temperatures. For example, Britain and Labrador in Canada are the same distance from the equator (they are the same latitude) but have very different climates. This is because a vast water current, called the Gulf Stream, transports warm water from the distant Gulf of Mexico to western Europe. This helps keep winter temperatures much warmer in Britain than they are in Labrador.

1 Fill the two painted jars with sand to about the same level. Screw the lids on firmly. Place both jars outside in the sunlight and leave them there for about two hours.

2 Now take the temperature of the sand in each jar. The sand in the black jar will be hotter than the sand in the white jar. Write down the temperatures in your notebook.

3 Now put the jars in the shade. Note the temperature of the sand in each jar every 15 minutes. The sand in the black jar will cool down faster than the sand in the white jar.

MEASURING
TEMPERATURE CHANGES

You will need: *two bowls, pitcher of water, sand, watch, thermometer, notebook, pen*

1 Pour water into one bowl and sand into the other bowl. You do not need to measure the exact amounts of sand and water—just use roughly equal amounts.

2 Place the bowls side by side in a cool place. Leave them for a few hours. Then note the temperature of the sand and water. The temperature of each should be about the same.

5 In this experiment, the sand acts like land and the water acts like ocean. The sand gets hot quicker than the water, but the water holds its heat longer than the sand does.

3 Then place the bowls side by side in the sunlight. Leave the bowls for an hour or two. Then measure the temperatures of the sand and water in each bowl.

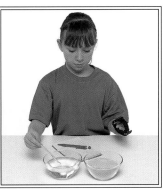

4 Then put each bowl in a cool place indoors. Record the temperature of the sand and water every 15 minutes. The sand cools down faster than the water.

Soaking up the sun
Reptiles such as crocodiles are cold-blooded. They rely on the surrounding temperature to keep warm. Their dark-colored skin helps them to absorb heat.

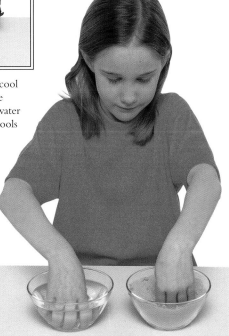

EL NIÑO AND LA NIÑA

GREAT masses of water are constantly on the move in all the world's oceans. They affect the climate of places along their path. For example, trade winds blow across the Pacific Ocean. Usually they are strong and blow from east to west. They drive a current of warm water westward.

Every few years the trade winds suddenly weaken and the whole system goes into reverse. A warm ocean current, called El Niño (Spanish for boy child), appears along the coast of Peru. This reversal in direction of the ocean current has an alarming effect on the weather, causing heavy rain and flooding in some areas but drought and forest fires in others. After a while, the trade winds usually regain their former strength and things return to normal.

Sometimes, however, the trade winds become much stronger than usual and drive the warm Pacific Ocean current much farther west than usual. This reverses weather patterns, creating droughts in normally wet regions and floods in normally dry ones. This strong reverse current is known as La Niña (girl child). Both El Niños and La Niñas seem to be happening more regularly. Scientists are still trying to figure out why this is so, but it could be caused by a gradual increase in the world's temperature, known as global warming.

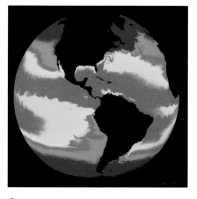

Ocean currents
A false-color map shows how the temperature varies across earth's oceans. The warmest areas are red, followed by yellow, green and light blue. The dark blue areas near the North and South poles are the coolest areas. North and South America are the distinctive black shapes in the middle of the picture. The temperature of the oceans is due to the absorption of heat energy from the sun. As the waters heat up, they begin to move and form oceanic currents. These currents are partly responsible for Earth's weather patterns.

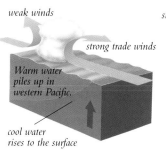

weak winds

strong trade winds

Warm water piles up in western Pacific.

cool water rises to the surface

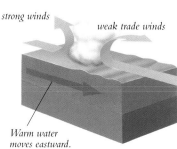

strong winds

weak trade winds

Warm water moves eastward.

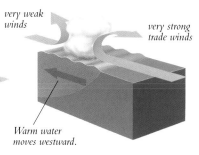

very weak winds

very strong trade winds

Warm water moves westward.

Normal conditions
In normal years, the steady trade winds of the tropical regions near the equator blow westward across the Pacific Ocean. They pick up moisture from the warm oceans and deliver rain to countries along the western Pacific Ocean.

El Niño
During El Niño years, the trade winds blowing westward across the Pacific Ocean become much weaker than usual. The warm surface waters of the Pacific Ocean are forced eastward by strong winds, which carry stormy weather systems.

La Niña
During La Niña years, the trade winds blowing westward become very strong indeed. The warm surface water of the Pacific Ocean is forced westward, leading to storms and much heavier rainfall than usual around the western Pacific Ocean.

Stormy beach

Houses just inland from Huntingdon Beach near Los Angeles, California, have been flooded by heavy rain. Precipitation (rainfall) levels in California are very much affected by El Niño years. The California coast is normally dry and sunny. El Niño may cause a vast increase in precipitation but may also give rise to drought here. The El Niño of 1982–3 was particularly destructive. The cost of the damage was estimated to be up to $13 billion.

Fire hazard

In 1998, forest fires raged out of control in Indonesia, in Southeast Asia. Usually, tropical rains blanket the islands of Southeast Asia, but El Niño was responsible for a huge drought and subsequent forest fires. More than 12,000sq mi. of forests were destroyed, creating clouds of smoke and haze that spread to neighboring countries such as Malaysia.

Bringing flood

El Niño has caused widespread flooding in Khartoum, the capital of Sudan in eastern Africa. The climate of Sudan is hot with seasonal rains during normal years. In El Niño years, however, the seasonal rains can be exceptionally heavy, flooding huge areas of land and making tens of thousands of people homeless.

Bringing famine

In the El Niño of 1997 and 1998, flooding devastated the crops in Sudan. Millions of people faced starvation and were forced to leave their homes. As a result of the flooding, relief agencies supplied food aid in camps such as this one.

BEATING THE HEAT

Weather and climate affect human life in many ways. More people live in warm climates than in colder climates. In some places, long dry spells, especially when accompanied by high temperatures, can lead to a shortage of food and even widespread starvation. In fact, parts of Africa have been in the grip of major drought and famine for decades.

Humans have developed a number of ways to avoid the effects of hot climates. Loose, light clothes help air to circulate around the body and protect the skin from sunburn, which can cause skin cancer. In the Mediterranean and parts of Asia, the walls of houses are very thick, keeping the house cool in the day and warm at night. Windows are small and covered with blinds or shutters to keep out the sun. The rooms are tall, so that the hot air rises to the ceiling.

Animals and plants from hot regions have adapted over time to cope with their surroundings and survive the heat.

Water shortage
When the weather is hot, the body needs plenty of water to avoid dehydration. When the body becomes too hot, it produces moisture in the form of sweat, which then evaporates into the air. This cools the skin and the blood beneath it.

The goat herders
Yemeni women in traditional dress lead a herd of goats to drink from a water supply in the Arabian Desert. Their hats and clothing cover their bodies and faces and protect their skin from the sun. If they become too hot, the rapid loss of water through sweating may lead to heat exhaustion. The symptoms of this include sickness, tiredness and fainting.

Saharan landscape
A Bedouin tribesman gazes out over the Sahara Desert in northern Africa, a region in which the temperature regularly exceeds 100°F. He wears loose, light-coloured clothing, which covers him from head to foot. The man's clothes allow the air to circulate around his body and also reflect the sunlight. This protects him from the sun's relentless heat.

Keeping cool

Running in and out of the spray from a garden sprinkler is a fun way to keep cool on a hot summer's day. Droplets of water from the sprinkler collect on the body and take heat away from the body as they evaporate. This makes the temperature feel lower than it actually is.

Desert survival

The camel is well adapted to life in its desert home. Its most famous feature is its fatty hump, which acts as a store of energy. This enables it to survive for many days without food and up to ten months without water. The camel produces very little urine, which cuts down water loss. The animal's thick fur also keeps it warm during the cold desert nights.

No sweat

The elephant's natural habitats are Africa and Asia. Its wrinkled and hairless skin retains water to help the animal cool down. The elephant does not sweat, but it can flap its two large ears to lose heat. The blood vessels in the ears are close to the surface of the skin and easily conduct heat away from the animal's body.

Prickly survivors

The huge trunk of the saguaro cactus is pleated like an accordion. After the rainy season, the stem absorbs water and the pleats unfold. A 19ft-tall cactus can store up to a ton of water in this way.

WHERE THE WEATHER IS

THE atmosphere is a layer of air that surrounds Earth. Most of the air molecules are near the surface of Earth. There are fewer air molecules the higher up you go, so the air is thinner there. At about 180 miles high, there are hardly any air molecules left in the atmosphere at all.

Earth's weather mostly takes place in a layer of the atmosphere called the troposphere. This layer is between 6 and 10 miles thick. It is in this layer that clouds form, rain and snow fall and thunder and lightning take place.

In the next layer up of the atmosphere, known as the stratosphere, there is a layer of a gas called ozone. This blocks harmful radiation from the sun. Recently, the ozone layer has been heavily damaged by harmful chemicals called pollutants, which include chlorofluorocarbons (CFCs). Despite a concerted worldwide effort to reduce their use, there is still deep concern that the ozone layer is thinning extremely rapidly. This thinning is especially noticeable over the North and South poles in spring.

A lot of hot air
Hot-air balloons float quietly above the Masai Mara National Reserve in East Africa. A hot-air balloon is powered by a gas burner, which heats up the air inside the balloon. Warm air rises, so warming the air inside the balloon makes that rise too.

Lights in the sky
Strange lights appear in the skies over the far north and far south, caused by particles from the sun colliding with gases in the atmosphere. In the north they are called the northern lights or the aurora borealis. In the south they are called the southern lights or the aurora australis.

Into outer space
The region where the molecules of Earth's atmosphere shoot off into space is sometimes referred to as the exosphere. This represents the upper limit of Earth's atmosphere and occurs at around 270-300mi. above the surface of the planet.

Red sky

In the evening, the sky often turns red or orange. This happens because when the sun is low in the sky, dust in the lower atmosphere scatters the blue light that we normally see. Only orange and red rays are left for us to see.

Blue sky

Skies appear blue because of the way light from the sun is scattered by the molecules of gas in the air. Dust, water droplets and other particles reduce the intensity of the colors. The bluest skies are seen when the air is at its purest, away from pollution in the cities. Many people who live in cities travel out to the countryside to take part in sports and leisure activities, such as windsurfing. Cleaner air can help people to feel more refreshed.

Mountain high

The peaks of mountains often rise high above the clouds. At the top of a mountain, there are far fewer molecules of air in the atmosphere than at the bottom. The air is thin and lacks oxygen. This affects the functions of the human body, causing a condition known as altitude sickness. This may affect climbers and walkers at heights of around 11,400ft and above. It causes feelings of sickness and light-headedness and, in severe cases, delusions or even death. This is the Aiguille Verte mountain in Chamonix, France, the peak of which is about 9,800ft.

IN THE AIR

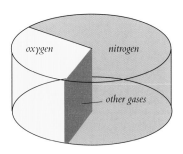

Gases in the air
About 78 percent of the air is nitrogen and 21 percent is oxygen The remaining 1 percent is gases such as carbon dioxide and argon.

MEASURING THE OXYGEN

You will need: *candle, clear mixing bowl, reusable adhesive, pitcher filled with colored water, glass jar, felt-tip pen*

THE air we breathe is made up of a mixture of different gases. Nitrogen makes up most of the air's volume, but oxygen is the most important gas, because most living things need a constant supply of it to stay alive. We can figure out the proportion of oxygen in the air in the simple experiment below. When things burn, they react with oxygen in the air and the oxygen is used up. As shown in the experiment below, if you burn a candle in a jar, you can use water to replace the oxygen that is used up. By noting how much water rises up the jar, you can estimate how much oxygen was in the jar to start with. You should find that the water level rises by about one-fifth, meaning that oxygen makes up about 20 percent of the air.

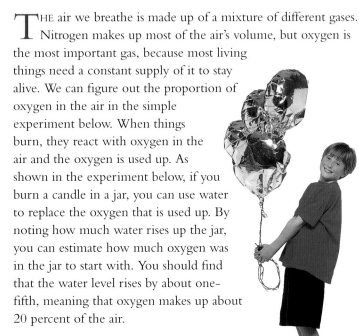

Up, up and away
A gas called helium can be used to inflate balloons. Helium-filled balloons float away quickly if you let go of their strings, because helium is lighter than the air.

1 Secure the candle to the bottom of the mixing bowl with reusable adhesive. Pour enough colored water in the bowl to fill it to a depth of about 1in.

2 Ask an adult to light the candle. As soon as it starts to burn, place the jar over the candle. Let the jar rest in the water on the bottom of the bowl and watch what happens.

3 The water rises from the bowl up into the jar until the candle goes out. Mark the water level on the jar—this will show how much oxygen was in the jar to start with.

SEE THE WEIGHT

You will need: *scissors, roll of tape, ruler, piece of thread, two balloons of the same size, balloon pump.*

1 Using your scissors, carefully cut a small piece off the roll of tape. Wrap the tape around the middle of the ruler. Cut a piece of thread and tie it to the tape on the ruler.

2 Lift up the ruler by the thread and see if you can balance it horizontally. You will need to adjust the position of the thread until the ruler balances.

3 Take a balloon and blow it up a little. Take the other balloon and blow it up to a much larger size than the first. Carefully tape the balloons to opposite ends of the ruler.

4 Hold up the ruler with the thread. The large balloon makes the ruler dip down at one end. It is heavier than the small balloon, because it contains more air.

FACT BOX

• All gases weigh something, but some gases are heavier than others. For instance, hydrogen is lighter than helium.

• If our atmosphere consisted only of hydrogen gas, the balloon filled with helium would sink rather than float away.

AIR ON THE MOVE

THE air in the atmosphere has weight. It pushes down on everything on earth with a force called atmospheric pressure. At sea level, atmospheric pressure is equivalent to the force of about 2.2 pounds on every half-inch of Earth's surface, but there are slight differences in atmospheric pressure from place to place. These differences make the air travel from a region of high pressure to a region of low pressure. This moving air is wind. Wind speed varies greatly, from a breeze (up to about 30mph) up to a hurricane (up to 180mph).

Breezes are gentle winds that often occur near the ocean where there is a difference in temperature between the sea and the land. The difference in temperature causes a difference in pressure and a breeze blows.

In contrast, large-scale wind systems blow all around the world, forming wind belts. These occur because of the differences in temperature between the hot equator and the cold polar regions. Earth is constantly rotating, and if this did not occur, the winds would blow from the high-pressure region over the cold poles to the low-pressure region near the equator. Since Earth rotates, however, this movement sets up a force called the Coriolis effect. This causes the wind to turn to the right of its path in the Northern Hemisphere and to the left of its path in the Southern Hemisphere. These two strong currents of air are called the trade winds, named because they once helped trading ships sail the oceans.

Sir Francis Beaufort
In 1805, English naval officer Sir Francis Beaufort (1774–1857) devised the scale that takes his name. The Beaufort scale soon became the standard method of estimating wind speeds, and it is still used today.

The Beaufort scale

The force, or strength, of the wind varies from place to place. The Beaufort scale is used to estimate the force of the wind. The scale is measured from Force 0, which means the air is not moving, to Force 12, which means a hurricane is blowing. One way you can guess the force of the wind is by the effect it has on you.

Force 0 on the Beaufort scale means that the wind speed is not noticeable. Smoke from a chimney rises vertically. When the wind reaches Force 2, you can feel the moving air on your face. This wind is called a breeze.

You can feel a Force 4 breeze pushing against your body when you walk.

| 0 | 1 | 2 | 3 | 4 | 5 |

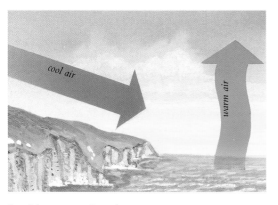

Land breezes and sea breezes
During the day, sea breezes are caused when the sun heats up the land, and it becomes warmer than the sea. The warm air rises above the land, pulling in cool air from the sea. The opposite (shown above) happens during the night, when a land breeze blows off the land.

Go fly a kite
A young girl flies a kite at the seaside. A kite flies when air moves past it. The movement of the air produces an upward force, called lift, on the kite. This force is responsible for supporting the weight of the kite and keeps it suspended in the air. The Chinese are thought to have invented the kite more than 2,300 years ago.

Wind power
Windmills were once used across Europe for milling (grinding) grain into flour. The enormous sails were powered by the wind. As the sails turned, they worked the machinery inside the mill.

Wind farm
Giant propellers harness the power of the wind at a wind farm in Altamont Pass in the United States. The propellers drive turbines that generate electricity for a nearby town.

At Force 7, the wind blows up to 30mph. You have to bend your body to walk against it.

At Force 9, the wind is known as a gale and blows at 50mph or more. You have to squat down, otherwise you will be blown over.

As the wind increases to Forces 10 and 11, you have to lie flat on the ground to stop yourself from being blown away. At Force 12, the wind is called hurricane force and causes widespread damage to everything that lies in its path.

6   7   8   9   10   11   12

AIR PRESSURE

THE weight of the air causes a force called air pressure to push down on the surface of Earth. Air pressure causes air to move in the atmosphere, because the molecules in the air always move from areas of high pressure to areas of low pressure.

Air pressure varies according to many factors, such as air temperature and air density (how tightly its particles are packed together). The molecules in cold air move slower than the molecules in warm air and they crowd closer together. Dense cold air contains lots of molecules and puts a greater force on Earth's surface.

Here are some tricks that involve air pressure. We can use the pressure of the air to knock over a pile of books. Sometimes paper can appear to be stronger than wood. This is due to the force of the air on the paper. In a fizzy chemical reaction, other gases, besides air, exert pressure on a balloon, forcing the balloon to expand.

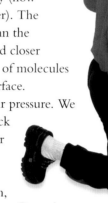

Pump it up
When you pump air into the tires of a bicycle, you increase the number of air molecules in each tire. The pressure of the air inside the tire also increases—the tyre feels hard after you have pumped it up.

FEELING THE PRESSURE

You will need: balloon, books, balloon pump, wooden strip, newspaper, thick protective glove

1 Place a balloon under some books. Blow air into the balloon using a balloon pump. As you pump, the air pressure inside the balloon rises. The increased force on the books pushes over the pile.

2 Cover the wooden strip with newspaper on a table. Leave a piece of the strip hanging over the end of the table. Wear a glove and strike the strip. Air pressure holds the paper in place, and the wood snaps.

CREATE AIR
PRESSURE

You will need: *funnel, bottle,
vinegar, balloon, baking powder*

1 Place the funnel in the neck of
the bottle. Carefully pour in
some of the vinegar, up to about
halfway. Make sure you wash the
funnel after you have used it.

2 Stretch the opening of the
balloon around the bottom of
the funnel. Carefully put some of
the baking powder into the funnel.
Shake the powder into the balloon.

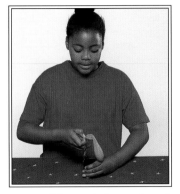

3 Carefully stretch the opening of
the balloon over the neck of the
bottle of vinegar. Let the powder–
filled part of the balloon hang down
to one side of the bottle.

4 Gently turn the balloon over,
so that the baking powder
goes into the vinegar. The
balloon expands as the
mixture starts to fizz.

5 The fizzing indicates that a chemical reaction
is taking place between the vinegar and the
baking powder. This reaction produces lots of a
gas called carbon dioxide. The pressure inside the
balloon rises as more carbon dioxide molecules
fill it. As a result, the increasing pressure of the
carbon dioxide forces the balloon to expand.

WHIRLWINDS AND TORNADOES

Whirling wind
Dust devils spring up on dusty land in hot, dry summers. They pick up dirt and carry it high into the sky. The wind rotates relatively slowly in a dust devil, and so does little if any damage.

WHEN you see leaves spinning around and around in the breeze, you are witnessing a miniature whirlwind. A similar thing happens on dusty land in the summer. Little whirlwinds pick up the dry dust and spin it around and upward into a spiraling column called a dust devil, which can climb up to 900-feet high.

Dust devils do little damage, but another kind of whirling wind is one of the most destructive forces in nature. It is a tornado, called twister because of its rapidly rotating winds. Tornadoes are born in violent thunderstorms. They form when a funnel-shaped column of whirling air forms beneath a thundercloud and descends to the ground. As it nears the ground, it picks up dust and debris. With winds racing around at speeds of up to 300mph, a tornado destroys everything in its path, ripping houses to pieces and tossing cars into the air. A typical tornado is about 300m across and moves across the ground at a speed of about 50km/h.

Tornadoes occur regularly on the flat central plains of the United States mostly along a broad path through Texas, Oklahoma, Kansas and Missouri. This area has become known as Tornado Alley. Tornadoes also form at sea, when they are called waterspouts. They are not as powerful and only last for only a few minutes.

A tornado is born
A huge thundercloud develops near Toronto, Canada. It is difficult to predict if a thunderstorm will give rise to a tornado, but meteorologists can tell where tornado-generating storms are most likely to form and will issue a tornado warning.

Sinister silhouette
The setting sun highlights the dark shape of a tornado in Colorado. The rapidly rotating column of air that touches the ground is known as the mesocyclone.

Fearful funnel
A dark, spinning funnel of a well-developed tornado heads for a town in Texas. If it hits the town, it will carve out a path of destruction several hundred yards across.

Furious freak
A freak tornado in Windsor Locks, Connecticut has left many houses in ruins. Tornadoes are most common in the Central Plains region of the US. Here, severe thunderstorms often develop, and these are ideal for the development of tornadoes.

Watch the waterspout
Waterspouts are much like tornadoes, but they occur over water rather than land. They are common in all equatorial oceans and inland seas. The water in the spout is formed by water vapor in the air condensing into water droplets. These are then pulled into the updraft within the cloud. Unlike tornadoes, however, waterspouts are usually rather weak storms and rarely cause much damage.

Tossed aside
Winds blowing at more than 180mph have hurled an aircraft onto a nearby barn during a tornado in Louisiana.

MEASURING THE WIND

THE wind shifts air from place to place and causes changes in the weather. Meteorologists chart the direction and speed of the wind to help them predict these changes. They use an instrument called a weather vane to find out the wind direction. Weather vanes are often made in the shape of cockerels, when they are called weather cocks. The project on this page tells you how to make a simple weather vane.

To measure the wind speed, meteorologists use a device called an anemometer. Most consist of a circle of cups that spin around when the wind blows, much like a windmill. The faster the wind blows, the faster the anemometer spins.

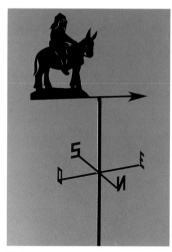

Going west
Weather vanes are commonly found on church steeples. This one points towards the east, which tells us that the wind is blowing from the east.

MAKE A WEATHER VANE

You will need: *reusable adhesive, plastic container and its lid, scissors, garden stick, plastic straws, colored card stock, pen, tape, pin, plywood, compass*

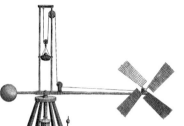

Ancient anemometer
The arm of this French anemometer from the 1600s moved when the wind blew against the propeller on the arm. The amount the arm moved was a measure of the wind speed.

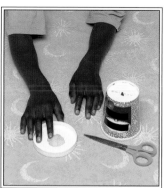

1 Stick a ball of reusable adhesive to the middle of the lid of the container. Ask an adult to pierce a hole in the bottom of the container. Place the container on the lid.

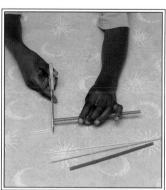

2 Slide the stick into one straw. Trim the end of the stick so that it is a little shorter than the straw. Push the straw and stick through the hole in the container and into the adhesive.

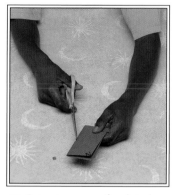

3 Cut out a square of card stock. Mark each corner with a point of the compass—N, S, E, W. Snip a hole in the middle of the card stock and slip the card stock over the straw.

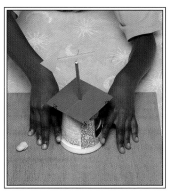

4 Cut out two card stock triangles. Stick them to each end of the second straw to form an arrow head and tail. Put a ball of adhesive in the top of the first straw in the container.

5 Push a pin through the middle of the arrow. Stick the pin into the reusable adhesive in the first straw. Be careful not to prick your finger when you handle the pin.

6 Secure your weather vane to a plywood base using a piece of reusable adhesive. Test it for use— the arrow should spin around freely when you blow on it.

7 When you have finished your weather vane, take it outside. Use a compass to make sure the corners of your weather vane point in the right directions. You can then use the weather vane to find out the direction the wind is blowing.

Windmills
The miniature windmills on the toy above spin faster the harder you blow on them. The sails of real windmills also spin faster as the speed of the wind increases. As a result windmills need a "governor" to regulate the speed of their rotation so that the sails are not damaged in strong winds.

Wind direction
Don't forget that the arrow points in the direction that the wind is blowing from. So if it points west, the wind is a west wind.

HURRICANES AND CYCLONES

THE whirling storms we call tornadoes are extremely powerful, but they are only a few hundred yards across and travel only a few miles. Much larger and more destructive are the great whirling storms called tropical cyclones. They form over the oceans of tropical regions. Gradually, they grow into great spirals of dense clouds as much as 300 miles across, with winds whirling around at speeds up to 180mph.

Tropical cyclones that form north of the equator and in the oceans around the US are called hurricanes. They are born in the warm waters of the Atlantic and east Pacific oceans and often affect the US and the Caribbean. Elsewhere in the world, hurricanes have other names. For example, typhoons form in the north Pacific Ocean and affect Japan.

When hurricanes hit land, they unleash heavy rain and howling winds that cause massive destruction. Strangely, in the centre of a hurricane there is a calm area about 18 miles across, called the eye, where there is little wind or clouds.

In a spiral
Space shuttle astronauts photographed a cyclone in the eastern part of the Pacific Ocean, off California, that covered hundreds of square miles.

Hurricane Gilbert
Although the high winds of a hurricane can inflict a great deal of damage, the majority of destruction is usually brought about by huge tidal waves and flooding. In September 1988, a total of 200 people died when Hurricane Gilbert slammed the Gulf Coast of Mexico.

One in the eye
An image taken by the crew of a space shuttle in November 1991 shows the clearly defined eye of a cyclone known as Typhoon Yuri. This typhoon formed near the Philippines in the eastern Pacific Ocean. Gradually, Typhoon Yuri grew to be more than 1,000 mi. in diameter. The clouds lining the wall of the typhoon extended to between 8 and 9 mi. deep. A typhoon of this huge size would give rise to winds with speeds of more than 150mph with sudden blasts (gusts) of over 165mph —a truly awesome spectacle of nature.

Mitch's mudslides
Although the high winds of a hurricane can inflict a great deal of damage, it is usually the huge waves and associated flooding that cause the most damage. Heavy rain following the passage of Hurricane Mitch caused huge mudslides in Tegucigalpa, Honduras, in late October 1998. In total, 17 people were killed as a result of the mudslides alone.

Andrew the destroyer
Some of the 200,000 or more homes and businesses in southern Florida, USA, that were destroyed or severely damaged by Hurricane Andrew in August 1992. The hurricane left 65 people dead, over 160,000 homeless and caused about $30 billion in damages.

Path of devastation
A time-lapse satellite image of Hurricane Andrew shows the path it took across the Atlantic Ocean and across southern Florida. The passage of the hurricane from right (August 23, 1992), to middle (August 24, 1992) and left (August 25, 1992) was monitored by meteorologists. Warnings were issued but, although important, they are not always able to save lives and property.

MASSES OF AIR

Great bodies of air, called air masses, are moving through the atmosphere all the time. These air masses can be huge, often covering whole continents or oceans. The way they move is complicated. It depends on the air pressure and the density of the air mass, and the Coriolis effect caused by Earth spinning around in space.

Air masses are associated with particular types of weather because they have certain temperatures and contain certain amounts of moisture. While a single air mass is passing us by, the weather remains the same. When another air mass takes its place with a different temperature and moisture, the weather changes. The worst weather occurs when a cold air mass and a warm air mass meet. Thick clouds form at this boundary, called a front. The weather settles down again after the front has passed by, that is, until another air mass replaces it.

Stormy weather
A storm may occur if two different air masses collide with one another. If a mass of warm air meets a mass of cold air, it produces widespread cloudiness and rain.

In the doldrums
Over the equator, the air is warm and the winds are light. Many years ago, sailing ships were unable to move for days when they came upon these regions, called the doldrums. However, storms can suddenly spring up in the doldrums due to the upward surge of moist air heated by the ocean.

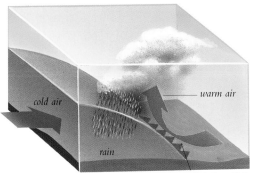

warm air

cold air

rain

symbols for cold front

Cold front
The meeting point between two air masses is called a cold front. It forms as a wedge of cool air pushes underneath a mass of warm air. The warm air is forced upward. As it cools, clouds form and rain falls.

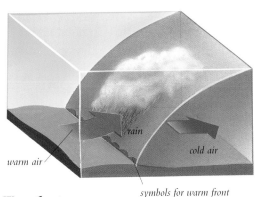

rain

cold air

warm air

symbols for warm front

Warm front
When a mass of warm air rides up over a mass of cold air, it causes a warm front. The rising of warm air over cold air, called over-running, produces clouds and rain well in advance of the front's surface boundary.

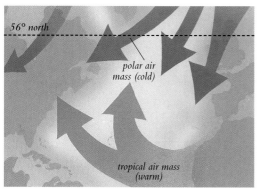

56° north

polar air
mass (cold)

tropical air mass
(warm)

Polar fronts

Great masses of warm and cool air move around Earth. Warm
air masses travel north and south away from the equator. Cold
air masses travel south and north away from the North and
South poles. As a mass of warm air travels toward the poles, it
encounters cold air moving down from the poles. The warm
and cold air masses do not readily mix and they are separated
by a boundary called the polar front. The polar front features
low air pressure, called the sub-polar low, where surface air
piles up and rises and storms develop. High in the sky, some of
the rising air moves back toward the equator, where it sinks
back to Earth's surface. This air then flows back toward the
poles and the process is repeated.

KEY

westerlies

trade winds

polar easterlies

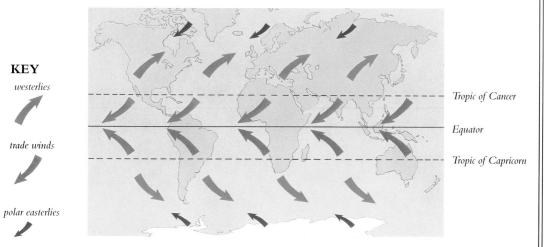

Tropic of Cancer

Equator

Tropic of Capricorn

World winds

This map shows the major movements of
air around the world. They are called wind
belts. The winds that blow in the belts are
prevailing winds, which means they nearly
always blow in the same direction. The
trade winds are warm because they blow
on either side of the equator. The westerlies
are cool and blow north of the Tropic of
Cancer and south of the Tropic of
Capricorn. The polar easterlies are icy and
blow around the North and South poles.

Fast winds

Sailing boats and ships rely on the trade winds
and westerlies to cross the oceans. In fact,
traders have relied on the trade winds for
thousands of years to transport their ships
across the Indian Ocean.

THE WATER CYCLE

Water moves around Earth and its atmosphere in a continuous process called the water cycle. Heat from the sun transforms water from oceans, lakes and rivers, into a gas, called water vapor, in a process called evaporation. In the atmosphere, water vapor rises, then cools and changes back into tiny droplets of liquid water. This is called condensation. Water droplets then gather together to form clouds. When water in the atmosphere is too heavy to be held in the air, it comes back to Earth's surface as precipitation— dew, rain, sleet or snow.

On the surface, water can be consumed by animals or taken up by plants. Plants use as much water as they need and then release the rest back into the atmosphere in a process called transpiration. Sometimes water sinks below Earth's surface to replenish underground supplies of water called groundwater. It can also remain on the surface in rivers and streams or lie frozen as glacial ice. Eventually, the water in lakes, rivers, streams and oceans evaporates once more to complete the water cycle.

Beneath the surface
When it rains, the water does not always flow into lakes, streams or oceans. Some disappears into the ground and becomes groundwater. In some places, this forms huge reservoirs of pure water hundreds of yards below the surface of Earth. Underground caverns form in limestone rock by the erosion (wearing away) of the rock by groundwater.

The water cycle
The Greek thinker Thales of Miletus (c.625–c.550 B.C.) was the first to describe the water cycle, over 2,500 years ago. The four main stages are evaporation, transpiration, condensation and precipitation. They form a continuous cycle.

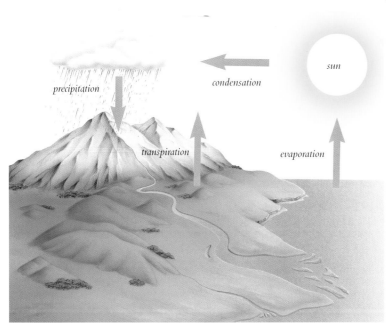
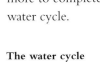

precipitation

condensation

sun

transpiration

evaporation

Elk in a fog

An elk looks lost in the early morning fog. When the visibility drops to less than ½ mi., the air is wet with tiny floating water droplets. This wet haze becomes a cloud resting near the surface of Earth and is called fog. It is formed when warm air full of water vapor moves in above cold ground. The vapor then condenses into droplets of water.

City in a smog

A reddish brown smog smothers Hong Kong. Smog is caused mainly by the exhaust gases from the motor vehicles that clog the city's streets. These gases contain unburnt particles, which combine with a gas called ozone to form the hazy smog.

Mountain stream

A stream runs through a valley in the Rocky Mountains. On the horizon, puffy white clouds drift toward the high peaks. As the clouds pass over the mountain peak they develop into rain clouds. As the clouds pass down the other side of the mountain, they shed their water in the form of rain or snow. This will feed the stream with a constant supply of water.

Turning to vapor

Sunlight streams through a hole in a thick cloud off Maui Island in the Pacific Ocean. The sun heats up water from the tropical ocean, and the water evaporates as a vapor in the air. As the vapor rises it cools and condenses, causing the cloud to grow.

HUMIDITY

WHY does 70°F in the Caribbean feel so much hotter than 70°F in Egypt? The answer is humidity—the air's water vapor content. When there is a lot of water vapour about, such as in the Caribbean, the air feels moist and sticky. This is because the perspiration on our skin cannot evaporate into the air very well—there is too much water in the air already. As a result, the perspiration stays on our skin and makes it wet, preventing us from cooling down. When there is little water vapor around, such as in Egypt, the air feels dry. The perspiration on our skin escapes into the air more easily.

Measuring the amount of water vapor in the air helps meteorologists forecast the weather. When the air is very humid, there is more chance that it will rain. Meteorologists use a device called a hygrometer to measure humidity. You could make a simple hygrometer using a long hair from your head. The length of hair changes as the humidity changes. This is the basis of an instrument called the hair hygrometer.

Another device meteorologists use to measure humidity is the wet–and–dry bulb thermometer, which contains two different thermometers. The difference in temperature between the two thermometers is used to calculate the humidity. You can make a simple hygrometer in this project.

Water producers
In the rainforests along the coast of northern California, it is warm and humid most of the time. Rainforests contain thousands of plants, all of which give off vast amounts of water from their leaves.

MEASURE THE HUMIDITY

You will need: *2 sheets of colored card stock, pen, scissors, glue, toothpick, used matchstick, straw, reusable adhesive, blotting paper, hole punch*

1 Cut out a card stock rectangle. Mark regular intervals along one side for a scale. Cut a ¼-in. slit in one short side. Split the parts out as shown above and glue them to a card stock base.

2 Cut another long rectangle from the first piece of card stock. Fold it and stick it to the card stock base as shown above. Pierce the top with a toothpick to form a pivot.

3 Attach the used matchstick to one end of the straw using some reusable adhesive to make a pointer. Both the matchstick and the adhesive give the pointer some weight.

4 Carefully cut out several squares of blotting paper. Use the hole punch to make a hole in the middle of each square. Slide the squares over the end of the pointer.

5 Now carefully pierce the toothpick pointer with the pivot. Position the pointer as shown above. Make sure the pointer can swing freely up and down.

Transpiring plants

Plants play a vital role in the transfer of water from the atmosphere to Earth. A plant's leaves give off water vapor in a process called transpiration. Cover a potted plant with a clear plastic bag, sealing the plastic around the pot with tape. Put the plant in direct sunlight for two hours. Notice that the bag starts to mist up and droplets of water form on the inside. They form when the water vapor given off by the plant turns back to a liquid.

6 Adjust the position of the toothpick so that it stays level. Take the hygrometer into the bathroom when you have a bath. The high humidity should make the blotting paper damp and the pointer will tip upwards. On a warm day outside, the blotting paper will dry and the pointer will tip down.

Building a sweat

Perspiration is the process by which we cool down. Heat is removed from the skin when water (sweat) evaporates from it. This process is less effective in humid weather when sweat remains on our skin.

LOOKING AT CLOUDS

Without clouds, there would be no rain, snow, thunder or lightning, and the sky would be very boring to look at. A cloud is a visible mass of tiny water droplets or ice crystals suspended in the air. Clouds can be thick or thin, big or little, and change form constantly.

They can be divided into four main types. Cumulus clouds are puffy masses that look like cotton balls. Stratus clouds are flat and often cover the entire sky, extending many hundreds of square miles. Cirrus clouds are wispy and form up to 8 miles above the surface of Earth. Dark clouds that bring rain are called nimbus. Cloud names can be combined. For example, cumulonimbus and nimbostratus are the names given to different clouds that produce rain.

Floating saucer
From a distance, this lenticular (lens-shaped) cloud looks much like a flying saucer. These clouds often form in waves that develop downwind of a mountain range. Lenticular clouds are often elongated and usually have well-defined outlines. Frequently, they form one above the other like a stack of pancakes.

cloud of ice crystals

cloud of water droplets

water vapour rises

How clouds form
When warm humid air rises and cools, the vapor turns into droplets of water and forms clouds. If the air is very cold, the vapor will turn into a cloud of ice crystals.

Cirrocumulus clouds
The small ripples in cirrocumulus clouds look much like the scales of a fish. The expression "mackerel sky" is used to describe a sky full of cirrocumulus clouds. These high white clouds are rounded and composed of ice crystals.

Cirrus clouds

The most common high clouds are the cirrus clouds, which are thin, wispy and made up of ice crystals. High winds can blow these clouds into long streamers called mares' tails.

Cumulus clouds

Puffy cumulus clouds take on a variety of shapes, but they most often look like cotton balls. They have round tops and, when they are dark and deep, they bring rain.

Cumulonimbus clouds

Cumulonimbus are thunder clouds. They are the largest clouds of all and form from cumulus clouds, often sprouting an anvil-shaped top, and produce heavy showers of precipitation.

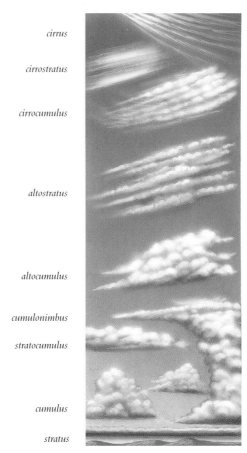

cirrus

cirrostratus

cirrocumulus

altostratus

altocumulus

cumulonimbus

stratocumulus

cumulus

stratus

Clouds at different heights

Clouds can be grouped according to how high they are above Earth's surface. High clouds include cirrus clouds. Altostratus and altocumulus are middle clouds. Stratus clouds are examples of low clouds.

The sun's halo

A spectacular halo around the sun is caused by a high cirrostratus cloud. Tiny ice particles in the cloud refract, or bend, light from the sun to create a luminous ring.

RAIN AND DEW

In SOME clouds, tiny water droplets remain suspended in the air. In other clouds, the droplets bump into one another and coalesce (join together). As the water droplets get larger and larger, they become too heavy to stay in the air. Eventually, the droplets fall out of the cloud as rain. Raindrops that reach Earth's surface are rarely larger than ¼ inch across.

Rain is the most common form of what meteorologists call precipitation. Precipitation is any form of water that falls from the atmosphere and reaches the ground. Dew is a form of precipitation. During a cold night, dew forms on surfaces such as leaves and the ground. The cold surfaces make the water vapor condense into droplets of liquid water.

Walk in the rain
It is fun to go out in the rain, but only if you dress properly. If you are wet, your body loses heat through your wet skin. If your body loses too much heat too quickly, a life-threatening condition called hypothermia may occur.

From small beginnings
Rain falls from the dark bottom of a cumulonimbus cloud over the hills in the distance. Cumulonimbus clouds start as small, fluffy white cumulus clouds. Then they begin to grow and develop a dark bottom. Cumulus clouds sometimes mushroom into massive thunderclouds that reach up to 9 mi. high and a severe thunderstorm may develop.

A dewy web
Dew drops glisten on a spider's web. The dew formed on the web when water vapor in the air cooled during the night and condensed as water droplets.

Rain to come
Dark, stormy nimbus clouds are piling up in the sky near Majorca in the Mediterranean. The clouds are low, and soon it will be raining hard.

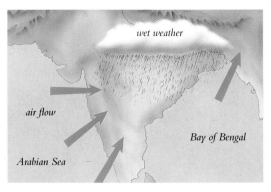

wet weather

air flow

Arabian Sea

Bay of Bengal

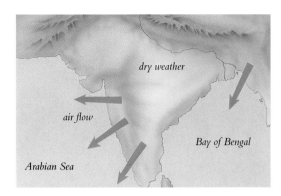

dry weather

air flow

Arabian Sea

Bay of Bengal

The summer monsoon

Some of the heaviest rain in the world falls in Asia during the monsoon period. During the summer, the air over the continent is warmer than the air over the water, and wind blows from the warm ocean. The winds bring heavy showers and thunderstorms, which can lead to flooding.

The winter monsoon

During the winter, the air over continental Asia becomes much colder than the air over the ocean. As a result, air flows out over the ocean. The winter monsoon provides southern Asia with generally fair weather and a dry season.

Railways into rivers

Days of almost continuous heavy summer monsoonal rains have turned this railway in Bangladesh into a river. The ground has become waterlogged, so the water will not drain away.

Moist air

In hot, tropical regions such as Hawaii, rain falls regularly throughout the year. Hawaii is surrounded by the Pacific Ocean. As a result, winds that blow from the sea to land bring air saturated (filled) with water vapor.

Summer burst

The monsoon rains fall across large areas of the tropics in summer, from northern Australia to the Caribbean. This monsoon rain is falling on a river in Indonesia.

MAKING RAINBOWS

RAINBOWS can often be seen during rainy weather when the sun is quite low in the sky. White sunlight is actually made up of a mixture of seven different colors— red, orange, yellow, green, blue, indigo and violet. Raindrops split up sunlight into a spread, or spectrum, of these separate colors to form a rainbow. The biggest rainbows form when the sun is low in the sky, so they are most commonly seen in the evenings or mornings. They are also less common in the tropics, where the sun is higher in the sky than in regions further north or south.

Other colored effects can be seen in the sky. Sometimes a circle made up of faint rainbow colors, called a halo, forms around the sun or the moon. Ice crystals in front of the sun or moon split up the sunlight into a spectrum.

White light can be split up into a colorful rainbow spectrum by shining it through a prism (a triangular wedge of glass). In the experiment, you can produce your own rainbow by shining light through a "wedge" of water.

Midday rainbow
The mist of water created by waterfalls, such as Victoria Falls on the border of Zambia and Zimbabwe, creates the perfect conditions for the formation of rainbows.

Splitting up white
If you shine white light through a prism, it splits up into different colors and emerges from the other side as a rainbow – a colored band called a spectrum.

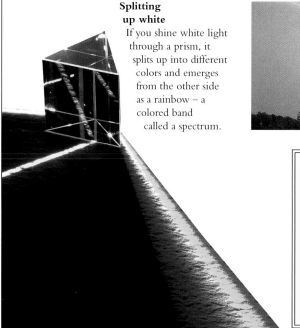

Split into seven
Rainbows are made up of seven different colors: red, orange, yellow, green, blue, indigo and violet. Here you can see a double rainbow.

FACT BOX

• White light is not really white. In fact, it is made up of seven different colors, as shown above. These colors combine to make white light.

• When light travels from air into water or glass (or back the other way) it is refracted, which means it bends. Different colors in the light bend more than others. Blue light bends most, red light least. As a result, the colors start to separate out and the result is a spectrum—the colors of the rainbow.

SPLIT LIGHT INTO A RAINBOW

You will need: *mirror, dish, reusable adhesive, pitcher of water, flashlight, piece of white card stock*

1 Carefully lean the mirror against the side of the dish. Use two small pieces of reusable adhesive to stick each side of the mirror to the dish at an angle.

2 Pour water into the dish until it is about 1½ in. in depth. As you fill the dish, a wedge-shaped volume of water is created alongside the mirror.

3 Switch on the flashlight. Shine the beam onto the surface of the water in front of the mirror. This should produce a spectrum or "rainbow."

4 It is best to do the next part of this experiment in dim light. Hold up the piece of white card stock stock above the dish to look at your rainbow. You may need to alter the positions of the card stock and flashlight before you can see it properly.

THUNDER AND LIGHTNING

A THUNDERSTORM occurs when warm, humid air rises. The upward air movement may be due to the uneven ground or temperature below. Huge, dark cumulonimbus thunderclouds develop overhead, flashes of lightning may fill the sky and the ground often trembles with a booming sound wave called thunder.

Lightning is a huge discharge of electricity. In a thundercloud, tiny drops of water and ice carry little bits of electricity, called electrical charges, which build up in parts of the cloud. In time, this charge becomes so great that electricity jumps to the ground or to other clouds, creating great sparks of lightning. The lightning heats up the air to a high temperature and makes it suddenly expand. This creates the explosion we hear as thunder.

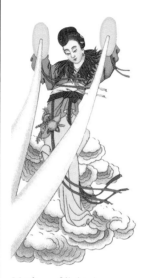

Mother of lightning
Sieou-wen-ing is a mythological character from ancient China. She is thought to be the mother of lightning. In this picture, she is sending bolts of lightning toward Earth.

Ice block
Hailstones are pieces of ice that fall from clouds. This one is 6 in. across. Most are much smaller, but they become bigger the longer they stay up in the clouds.

Flashes of lightning
Lightning illuminates the night above the distant mountains. Light travels so fast that we see a flash of lightning almost instantly. The sound of thunder takes much longer to reach our ears, however, because sound waves travel more slowly than light. Sometimes, lightning is seen but no thunder is heard. This happens because during a thunderstorm, the air moves erratically and often scatters the sound waves. As a result, the thunder cannot be heard.

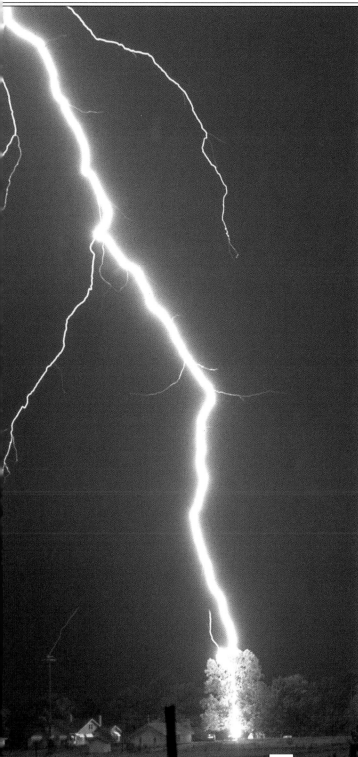

Lightning conductor
An experimental lightning conductor helps scientists study lightning. Electricity is easily conducted (passed along) through metal. Many tall buildings have a metal rod at the top. If lightning strikes, the metal conducts the electricity safely to the ground, and the building will not be damaged.

Struck by lightning
Lightning has struck a tree and left a trail of exposed wood in the bark. Lightning bolts often strike tall objects such as trees and buildings.

Bolt from the blue
A powerful streak of lightning discharges from thunderclouds and strikes a tree. The air surrounding lightning often rises to 54,000°F and may set the whole tree on fire.

CHARGING UP

THE lightning that flashes in the sky during a thunderstorm is not the same kind of electricity that makes your television or radio work. Lightning is a form of static electricity, which is made up of tiny electrical charges. These little bits of electricity can build up to create a much bigger charge, or voltage. Unlike ordinary electricity, the electrical charge does not usually flow away, which is why it is called static (not moving) electricity. In a thundercloud, the static electricity builds up so much that the air cannot hold it, and it jumps around as lightning flashes. In these experiments, you can build up small electrical charges by rubbing things together.

MAKE STATIC ELECTRICITY

You will need: balloons, balloon pump, hairbrush.

Van de Graaff generator
If you put your hands on a device called a Van de Graaff generator, your hair stands on end. A belt of material carries tiny electrical charges, which build up on a metal sphere, making static electricity.

1 Blow up a number of balloons with a balloon pump. Rub the balloons against a sweater or something made from wool. Put the balloons in different places.

2 Put the balloons on the ceiling, on the walls and even on your friends. The tiny electrical charges that form static electricity will make the balloons "stick" to things.

3 You can make your hair charge up with static electricity, too. Brush your hair when it is dry. Then hold the hairbrush near your hair. It will make your hair stand on end.

JUMPING ELECTRICITY

You will need: *sheet of plastic, tape, rubber gloves, metal dish, fork*

If you put your hands over a plasma ball, little bolts of electrical charge move like lightning toward your hands. The "lightning" consists of harmless flashes of static electricity, traveling in a plasma (sea) of electrified particles.

1 Lay out the sheet of plastic on the table and secure the edges with tape. This prevents the sheet from sliding around and disrupting your experiment.

2 Put the rubber glove on one hand. Slide the metal dish back and forth over the plastic sheet for a few minutes. This will charge the dish with static electricity.

3 Hold the fork with your ungloved hand. As you bring the fork close to the dish, you should see a spark jump. It is easier to see this in the dark.

FLOOD AND DROUGHT

Playtime
The flooded streets of Pahang, Malaysia, are a playground for some, but most people are mopping up the water after it has swept through their houses.

FLOODING (too much water) and drought (too little water) can have a devastating effect on the environment. The people who live in areas prone to these extreme weather conditions have to cope as best they can.

In some parts of the world, flooding occurs regularly in certain seasons, such as during the summer monsoons in India. Sometimes, flooding can be caused by cyclones. In February 2000, a cyclone with winds blowing at up to 161 mph caused widespread flooding in Mozambique. Tens of thousands of people were killed or made homeless as vast areas of land became submerged in water. Sudden flooding following heavy rains can be equally destructive. In December 1999, prolonged rain created terrible mudslides that buried or swept away whole towns and villages along the northern coast of Venezuela.

At the same time, east Africa was suffering from severe drought. Two years had passed without the usual seasonal rains. The crops had failed, livestock were dying in their thousands and much of the population was suffering from malnutrition.

Breaking records
A weather satellite image reveals the extent of the flooding of the Missouri and Mississippi rivers in July 1993. The city of St. Louis is colored purple at the bottom of the picture. In the summer of 1993, the American Midwest suffered the worst flooding since records began. River levels rose up to 150 ft above normal.

A dangerous delta
A Bangladeshi family stands by the remains of their home after a devastating storm in the Ganges Delta. A cyclone has surged inland from the Indian Ocean, crossed the flat Delta region and flattened everything in its path.

Around the waterhole
Animals gather around a waterhole during the dry season on the east African savanna. During the dry season no rain falls at all. All the water dries up, and the vegetation available for the animals to graze on gets scarcer. Only a few waterholes are left, but even these will shrink as the sun relentlessly beats down on the plains.

Death in the drought
In 1992, parts of east Africa suffered one of the worst droughts ever recorded. Crops were devastated, and livestock such as cattle were killed by the thousand.

Dry and lifeless
These trees have died through lack of water. Drought is caused by a lack of precipitation, but it can also be caused by hot, dry winds and frequent fires. These elements combine to take moisture from the soil and use up groundwater beneath the top levels of the soil.

Aid for Ethiopia
Families from Ethiopia in east Africa gather at an aid center to collect food. Ethiopia is one of the world's poorest countries. Most people live by farming the land, but drought results in a very poor harvest and widespread famine. In 1984, more than 800,000 people are known to have died in one of the worst droughts seen to date.

GAUGING THE RAIN

THE amount of precipitation (rain, sleet, snow or dew) that falls from the atmosphere varies widely throughout the world. Heavy rain falls regularly in tropical regions around the equator. Here, the air contains plenty of moisture evaporated from the warm oceans. The summer monsoon rains that occur over southern Asia can reach record amounts. Cherrapunji in northeastern India receives an average of 30 feet of rainfall each year, most of which falls during the summer monsoon between April and October. These rains are essential to the agriculture of southern Asia. Since so many people depend on the monsoon to survive, meteorologists need to predict how much rain will fall so that food crops will grow.

How much rainfall do you get where you live? Make this simple rain gauge to measure the amount. Meteorologists use a similar rain gauge at many weather stations around the world. If it is very rainy where you live, this project will keep you busy, but if you live in a desert region, you may have to wait a long time for any rain!

Keeping dry
Umbrellas were probably invented in China as early as the 2nd century B.C.

MEASURING RAINFALL

You will need: scissors, tape, large jar (such as a candy jar), ruler, ballpoint pen, large plastic funnel, tall narrow jar or bottle, notebook

1 Cut a piece of tape to the height of the jar and stick it on. Mark a scale on the tape at ½ in. intervals. Measure the diameter of the jar, and cut the funnel to the same size.

2 Place the funnel in the jar. Put the gauge outside in an open space away from any trees. Look at the gauge at the same time each day. Has it rained in the last 24 hours?

3 If it has rained, use the scale to see how much water is in the jar. This is the rainfall for the past 24 hours. Make a note of the reading. Empty the jar before you return it to its place

Being more precise

Measure rainfall more accurately by using a separate narrow measuring jar. Cut a length of tape to the height of the narrow jar and stick it to the side. Pour some water into the large collecting jar up to the ½ in. mark. Now pour this water into the smaller measuring bottle. Mark ½ in. where the water level reaches. Divide the length from the bottom of the bottle to the ½ in. mark into 10 equal parts. Each mark you make will be equivalent to 1mm of rainfall. Extend the scale past the ½ in. mark to the top of the measuring bottle.

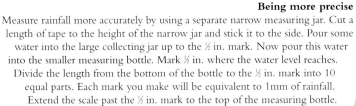

All-in-one weather instrument

You can buy an all-in-one weather instrument, which measures temperature, rainfall, wind direction and wind speed. These are handy if you don't have much space to set up lots of equipment.

Automatic weather station

Meteorologists use all-in-one weather instruments to measure different features of the weather. These instruments automatically monitor local weather conditions, such as wind speed and direction, air pressure, temperature, humidity and solar radiation.

FACT BOX

• The wettest place in the world is Mawsynram in India. Here, an average of almost 40 ft of rain falls every year.

• New York and Sydney have a little over 3 ft of rain a year. Paris and London have about 24 in. a year.

• The driest place in the world is the Atacama Desert, west of the Andes in Chile, South America. In parts of the desert just a few showers fall every 100 years.

• Sea storms can cause worse flooding than rainfall. The large waves that form can submerge coastal areas.

SNOW AND ICE

Snow falls in winter in many countries. It also falls all year round in places near the North and South poles and at the top of mountains. Most of the precipitation that actually reaches the ground starts as snow. At the top of high clouds the temperature is below the freezing point of water, and ice crystals form. Ice crystals join together to form snowflakes that fall from the clouds when the snowflakes become too heavy. If the lower air is warm, however, the snowflakes will melt and turn into rain. A mixture of snow and rain sometimes falls as sleet. This occurs when the falling snowflakes start to melt and then turn back into ice as they pass through a freezing layer of air.

On many winter nights the ground becomes snow-white even when it has not been snowing. This white covering is called frost, which forms when the ground gets cold and water vapor in the air condenses on it. The water immediately freezes into tiny sparkling crystals of ice.

Works of art
Snowflakes are made up of masses of tiny ice crystals. Under a microscope, the most common snowflake form is a branching star shape called a dendrite.

Death in the valley
In February 1999, an avalanche devastated a village in the Chamonix Valley in the French Alps. About 40,000 tons of snow hurtled down the mountain slopes at 125 mph. The snow buried houses and cars, killing 12 people.

Avalanche!
Thousands of tons of snow break loose in an avalanche on Mount Everest in the Himalayas. Avalanches career downhill at tremendous speeds, destroying everything in their path. They occur when the weight of the snow on the mountain exceeds the forces of gravity and friction that hold the snow in place.

Ice on glass

Ice crystals have formed on a windowpane. If glass gets very cold, water vapor in the air condenses on it, forming crystals where it freezes.

Jack Frost

Jack Frost is a mythical character who is thought to make the beautiful icy patterns you find outside on trees, plants and fences during cold weather.

Chunks of ice

Most of the ice in the world is found in the ice caps in the Arctic and Antarctic. Around 3.7 million sq mi. of ice cover the Arctic Ocean in the north. This huge ice pack is broken into large floes (sea ice) by the wind and ocean currents. Antarctica is covered by a permanent ice cap, which is over 1½mi. thick at the center of the continent.

Ice storms in Quebec

During the winter of 1998, the province of Quebec in Canada suffered a storm of icy rain that lasted for a whole week. Ice up to 3 in. thick collected on trees, electricity pylons and cables. The ice was so heavy that trees and pylons collapsed, resulting in widespread damage and disruption. The more remote areas of Quebec did not have any electricity for a month. Many farmers lost livestock because they could no longer feed them or keep them warm. This was the worst ice storm experienced in this region for at least 100 years.

COPING WITH COLD

Needle leaves
The needle-like leaves of these conifers in the Rocky Mountains of North America lose much less heat than broad leaves would.

O NLY a tiny proportion of animals and plants live in the cold temperate regions in the far north of North America, Europe and Asia and in the polar regions around the North and South poles. In these areas the winters are long, and temperatures often fall below −58°F. The plants and animals that live in these bitterly cold parts of the world are well adapted to the environment. The main plants are evergreen conifer trees. These form a great northern, or boreal, forest region that spans the continents of North America, Europe and Asia.

The largest animals of the boreal forests are caribou and moose (elk). These animals have thick fur and can survive on almost any type of vegetation. They shelter in the forests in the winter but venture onto open ground farther north in summer. This open ground is called the tundra, which is covered by snow and ice for most of the year. A few yards below the surface, the ground is permanently frozen. It is too cold for trees to grow, so grasses and low shrubs make up the vegetation. These plants make the most of the short summer months by growing, flowering and seeding rapidly.

Farther north still, on the permanently frozen north polar ice cap, plants do not grow. Polar bears hunt seals that swim in the icy waters of the Arctic Ocean. Polar bears have thick fur with a layer of fat underneath to protect their bodies against the cold. Seals and whales have a thick layer of blubber beneath the skin to insulate them from the cold. Seals and whales are also found around Antarctica at the opposite end of Earth.

Blubber is best
Seals spend a lot of time swimming in the ice-cold waters of the Arctic and Antarctic oceans. Seals are warm-blooded, which means they can regulate their own body heat. Under their skin, a fat-filled layer of spongy tissue, called blubber, insulates their bodies from the cold.

Penguin playground
Adelie penguins gather on the ice along the coast of Antarctica. The temperatures can drop to as low as −130°F in Antarctica. Penguins are protected from the severe cold by their closely packed, oily feathers and an insulating layer of fat under their skin.

Saami in the snow

A caribou herder from Kataukeino in northern Norway relaxes on his snow scooter during the spring migration of caribou. He is one of the Saami people from northern Scandinavia, and is dressed in traditional clothing—a parka and trousers made out of animal skins and trimmed with fur. These warm clothes will insulate him against the bitter cold of the Scandinavian tundra.

Fruit of the tundra

Arctic plants flower when the ground is barely free of snow, taking advantage of the short summer. The ground over the permanently frozen layer of soil, called permafrost, thaws in the summer. The plants then get a roothold. They cannot develop deep roots because of the solid layer of permafrost.

Like father, like son

An Inuit father and his son live in the Northwest Territories of Canada, which has one of the coldest climates on Earth. Their bodies are well adapted to the climate. They are short, stocky and their faces have grown used to the cold. Inuit people have a very fatty diet to build up a thick layer of fat.

The treeless tundra

It is summer and the lower slopes of the mountains in Denali National Park, Alaska, have lost their covering of snow. Although the ground just below the surface is still frozen, plants such as grasses and low shrubs can still survive.

ICE AGE OR GREENHOUSE?

Ball of fire
A shooting star, or meteor, streaks through the atmosphere. Shooting stars are streaks of light created when lumps of rock and dust hurtle towards Earth and burn up in Earth's atmosphere. Parts of a rock often fall to the ground as meteorites. If a large meteorite hits Earth enough material can be thrown into the atmosphere to bring about a change in climate. This may have caused the extinction of the dinosaurs some 65 million years ago.

Throughout the history of Earth, the climate has undergone many changes. Over the past million years or so, the climate has alternated between periods of warmth and cold. During the cold periods, called ice ages, most of North America and Europe became covered in vast sheets of ice. The last cold period lasted until about 25,000 years ago. Scientists used to think that another ice age was approaching. In fact, the atmosphere has been warming at a dramatic rate since the 1970s. This is due to a number of reasons.

Most importantly, humans are burning more and more fuels, such as coal and oil, which creates carbon dioxide. This gas is building up in the atmosphere, trapping the sun's heat. As a result, the atmosphere acts much like a greenhouse. As more and more carbon dioxide builds up in the atmosphere, this so-called "greenhouse effect" warms the climate. Scientists think that if humans continue to produce carbon dioxide by burning fossil fuels, Earth's climate will warm by several degrees in the next 50 years. This may make the polar ice caps melt, causing sea levels to rise and flooding many countries. Rising temperatures also alter wind patterns and ocean currents, disrupting weather patterns and climates throughout the world.

Holding back the tides
The Thames Flood Barrier at Woolwich in London will prevent the city from being flooded in case of an exceptionally high tide. If the greenhouse effect becomes a reality, this preventative measure may save millions of people who live in the city.

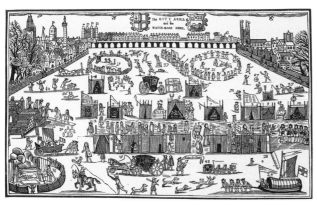

Frozen over
A change in the heat output of the sun may have caused the Little Ice Age that occurred in the 1600s. During this time, the River Thames in London froze so hard that a series of frost fairs could be held on it. The picture above shows the Frost Fair that was held in 1683.

The ash clouds of Pinatubo

After lying dormant (sleeping) for more than 500 years, the volcano Mount Pinatubo erupted in June 1991. As the volcano erupted, it threw vast clouds of ash high into the air, blocking light from the sun for days. Torrential rains followed the eruption and caused mud and ash slides, which devastated the surrounding countryside. Ash particles in the atmosphere were also responsible for cooler summers around the world for several years.

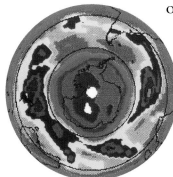

Ozone hole

In the 1980s, scientists discovered that the ozone layer, part of Earth's atmosphere, was thinning over Antarctica. If the ozone layer becomes too thin, it will let more rays through from the sun, which will harm Earth.

Cycle safely

A cyclist wears a protective face mask to filter out the harmful fumes of busy city traffic. Gases released by car engines are now known to be responsible, in part, for the greenhouse effect.

SOHO image

The SOlar Heliospheric Observatory (SOHO) space probe took this picture of the scorching surface of the sun. Using space observatories such as these, meteorologists learn more about how and why changes take place in the sun's energy output.

STUDYING THE WEATHER

METEOROLOGISTS do two main jobs. They collect data and process information about the weather from day to day. Then they use this information to help them forecast future weather trends. Meteorologists collect information from weather stations scattered all over the world. They use a variety of measuring instruments. Thermometers measure the temperature, barometers measure air pressure and hygrometers measure the humidity of the air. Weather vanes show the direction of the wind and anemometers measure its speed.

Increasingly meteorologists are turning to space technology to help them. They send weather satellites into orbit to take pictures of clouds and measure weather conditions in the air. Satellites are useful because they can record weather in remote regions where there are no weather stations.

Blast-off
A rocket blasts off from Cape Canaverel, Florida. The rocket is carrying a weather satellite that will orbit Earth and send images to meteorologists back on Earth, along with other weather data.

Cloud in the north
A number of satellite pictures have been joined together to give a true color image of Earth. The polar ice cap at the North Pole is shown at the top here. Thick cloud covers the pole and reaches into the North Atlantic Ocean.

Ready for launch
A meteorologist launches a weather balloon at the Kourou Space Center in South America. The weather balloon will be tracked once it is in the air. The direction it travels will indicate the wind's direction. Readings of temperature and humidity from the instruments it carries will also be sent back.

Measuring sunshine

A sunshine recorder is made up of a glass ball that acts like a lens. When the sun shines, the glass ball focuses the light onto a sheet of paper below the ball. The focused light leaves a scorch mark on the paper that is matched to a calibrated time scale. In this way, the meteorologist can record how long the sun shines each day.

Weather at sea

An automatic weather buoy carries many types of weather-recording devices, such as anemometers, barometers, hygrometers and thermometers. The readings from the different instruments are transmitted by radio to weather stations or passing satellites.

Head for the clouds

A pilot flies his plane straight into a storm. He works for the National Weather Service. The plane is a specially strengthened aircraft that can cope with violent air currents, lightning and bombardment by hailstones. Instruments beneath the wings monitor weather conditions.

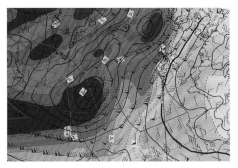

Storm map

A computer map is used to predict the likelihood of a storm in the Atlantic Ocean. The solid lines are called isobars and link regions of equal air pressure. Storms often occur in regions where the isobars are close together.

Computer forecasting

Meteorologists use computers to predict how the weather will change. This can help them make more accurate forecasts.

YOUR WEATHER STATION

Meteorologists work at about 12,000 weather stations worldwide, gathering information about the weather. They feed the data they gather from satellites, balloons, weather buoys and other instruments into powerful computers to provide them with an overall view of the weather and how it may change. Using this information, they can draw weather maps that show the state of the weather at any one time, using symbols to represent conditions such as rainfall, wind direction and pressure. They also use this information to draw other charts that they use to make a forecast of the weather.

You can set up your own weather station to record weather conditions with a few simple instruments. You will be able to use some of the instruments you have made in earlier projects, such as the weather vane, hygrometer and rain gauge. In addition, you will need to buy a thermometer and a barometer (which measures air pressure), both of which can be bought fairly inexpensively.

How hot is it?
A thermometer must always be kept in the shade to measure the air temperature accurately. If the device is left in direct sunlight, the liquid will also absorb energy from the sun. As a result, the thermometer will indicate a temperature higher than the actual air temperature.

Pine station
No home weather station would be complete without pine cones. When they are ripe, pine cones open on dry days to release their seeds. They close up if the weather is humid or damp.

Make a note
Take measurements with your weather instruments every day. Write them down in a special weather book. Also, make a note of what the weather is like generally—fine, cloudy, drizzle, frosty and so on. Don't forget to make a note of the date!

How much did it rain?
Your rain gauge will tell you this. Measure the amount of water in the jar. Use the measuring bottle to be more accurate. Always empty the jar when you have finished.

Dry or damp

Seaweed is a useful item to have in your weather station. Like pine cones, seaweed changes as the humidity changes. If the weather is dry, the seaweed feels dry and brittle. If the weather is humid, however, the seaweed feels flexible and damp.

Cumulus clouds

As well as using the instruments you have made to predict what the weather will be like, you can make general predictions, too. Studying the clouds is often a good way of telling what sort of weather is in store. Puffy cumulus clouds that grow in size and turn darker suggest that there could soon be showers. However, these clouds are scattered, so the showers will not last for long.

Red skies

Red clouds at dawn is often a sign that rain is on the way. A red sky at night, however, can be a good sign, promising that the next day will be fine. An old saying sums this up with the words "Red sky at night, sailor's delight. Red sky in the morning, sailor's warning."

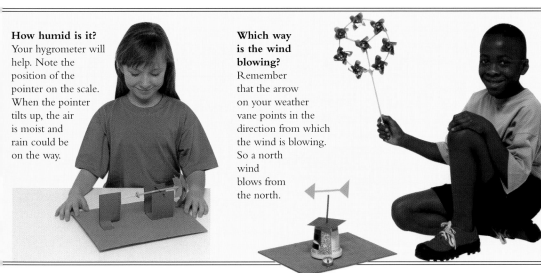

How humid is it?

Your hygrometer will help. Note the position of the pointer on the scale. When the pointer tilts up, the air is moist and rain could be on the way.

Which way is the wind blowing?

Remember that the arrow on your weather vane points in the direction from which the wind is blowing. So a north wind blows from the north.

GLOSSARY

anemometer
An instrument used in weather forecasting to measure the speed and force of the wind.

atmosphere
The layer of gases that surrounds a planet and is held to it by the planet's gravity (force of attraction).

atmospheric pressure
A measure of the weight of the atmosphere pressing down on the surface of the Earth.

barometer
An instrument used in weather forecasting to measure the pressure of the atmosphere.

Beaufort scale
A range of code numbers that is used to describe the force of the wind, from 0 (calm) to 12 (hurricane force). The Beaufort scale is named after British naval officer Sir Francis Beaufort, who formulated it.

Celsius scale
A scale for measuring temperature where 0 degrees is assigned to the temperature at which water freezes and 100 degrees to the temperature at which water boils. The scale was introduced by Swedish astronomer Anders Celsius.

climate
The general pattern of the weather of a place, year by year.

condensation
The process by which water vapor becomes a liquid.

Coriolis force
A theoretical force that results from Earth's rotation in space. The Coriolis force causes moving particles, including the wind, to deflect to the right in the Northern Hemisphere and to the left in the Southern Hemisphere.

cyclone
An area of low pressure into which winds spiral clockwise in the Southern Hemisphere and counterclockwise in the Northern Hemisphere. This weather condition is usually associated with a violent tropical storm.

dew
Water that condenses on objects near the ground when they are much cooler than the surrounding air.

doldrums
The region near the equator that is characterized by low pressure and light, shifting winds.

drought
A long time without rain, when living things do not have the water they need.

dust devil
A small, rapidly rotating wind that is visible due to the dust it picks up from the ground as it rotates.

El Niño
A major ocean-warming event that begins along the coast of Peru and triggers weather extremes, which happen once every three to seven years.

equator
The imaginary circle around the middle of Earth between the North and South poles. This region has a climate that stays hot all year round because it always gets the greatest amount of direct sunlight as Earth turns on its axis.

exosphere
The outermost layer of Earth's atmosphere that forms a boundary with space.

Fahrenheit scale
A scale for measuring temperature at which 32 degrees is assigned to the temperature at which water freezes and 212 degrees to the temperature at which water boils. The scale was formulated by Gabriel Daniel Fahrenheit.

front
The point or boundary where two air masses that have different temperatures and different amounts of moisture meet. When two fronts meet, there is a change in the weather.

greenhouse effect
The way certain gases in Earth's atmosphere trap the sun's heat like the panes of glass in a greenhouse. The effect increases the temperature of Earth's surface and lower atmosphere.

Gulf Stream
A warm, swift, narrow ocean current flowing along the east coast of the United States and toward western Europe.

halo
Rings that encircle the sun or moon when seen through a cloud composed of ice crystals or a sky filled with ice crystals. The effect is due to the refraction of light.

humidity
A measure of the amount of water, or moisture, in the air.

hurricane
A severe tropical cyclone with wind speeds of over 75 mph.

hygrometer
An instrument used in weather forecasting to measure humidity.

land breeze
A gentle wind that blows from the land toward the sea.

La Niña
An event in which the central and eastern tropical Pacific Ocean turns cooler than normal.

mesosphere
The layer of Earth's atmosphere between the stratosphere and the thermosphere.

meteorologist
A person who studies the science of meteorology (weather study) and forecasts and reports on the weather.

meteorology
A science that studies the atmosphere, climates and weather conditions in regions throughout the world.

monsoon
A wind that reverses its direction in winter and summer. Monsoon winds commonly affect southern Asia around the Indian Ocean, often bringing heavy rains in the summer season.

ozone
A form of oxygen that exists in a layer of Earth's atmosphere that blocks dangerous rays from the sun.

precipitation
Any form of water (rain, sleet, hail or snow) that comes out of the air and falls to the ground.

prevailing winds
The wind direction most frequently observed during a given period.

radiosonde
A scientific instrument carried high into the air, usually by a weather balloon. The radiosonde sends information back to Earth about the atmosphere and weather conditions.

satellite
A spacecraft that circles around Earth in orbit. It sends information back to scientists on Earth to help them study the world's climates and weather.

savanna
A huge region of grassland typically found in a tropical climate.

sea breeze
A gentle wind that blows from the sea toward the land.

spectrum
The spread of colors found in white light in the order red, orange, yellow, green, blue, indigo and violet. A spectrum appears when white light passes through a prism (a transparent solid object such as a wedge of glass) or through raindrops to form a rainbow.

stratosphere
An upper layer of Earth's atmosphere, above the clouds.

thermosphere
A layer of Earth's atmosphere above the mesosphere, beginning about 50 mi. above Earth's surface.

tornado
An intense, rapidly rotating column of air that extends from a thundercloud in the shape of a funnel.

transpiration
The process in the water cycle by which plants release water vapor into the air. The vapor will eventually turn back into liquid and fall back to Earth as some form of precipitation.

tropics
Part of Earth's surface that lies between the Tropic of Cancer (at a latitude of 23.5 degrees north of the equator) and the Tropic of Capricorn (at a latitude of 23.5 degrees south of the equator).

troposphere
The layer of Earth's atmosphere closest to the surface of Earth, where clouds form.

tundra
A huge treeless area in the Arctic region that has very long, harsh winters and where the ground beneath the surface is always frozen, even in the summer.

typhoon
A hurricane that forms over the western Pacific Ocean.

waterspout
A column of rotating wind over water that has characteristics of a dust devil and a tornado.

weather
The condition of the atmosphere at any particular time and place.

wind
Air moving in relation to Earth's surface.

INDEX

A
air 18-22
air masses 32-3
air pressure 22-5, 59
altitude 11, 12, 19
anemometers 28
animals 10-11, 13, 17, 49, 54
atmosphere 6, 18-20
atmospheric pressure 22
aurora australis 18
aurora borealis 18
avalanches 52

B
barometers 60
Beaufort scale 22-3
breezes 22, 23

C
cacti 17
carbon dioxide 20, 56
cirrus clouds 38-9
climate 10-11, 12, 14, 16, 41
climate changes 56
climatic zones 10-11
clouds 6, 30-1, 34-5, 38-40, 52
cold, adaptation to 54-5
cold fronts 32
cold temperate climates 10-11
computers 59
condensation 34-5, 40
Coriolis effect 22, 32
cumulus clouds 38-9, 40, 61
cyclones 30-1, 48

D
dehydration 16
deserts 5, 10, 11, 16-17, 51
dew 40
doldrums 32
droughts 14-15, 48-9
dust devils 26

E
El Niño 14-15
electricity 44-7

electromagnetic radiation 6
equator 6, 10, 32-3
evaporation 34-5

F
famine 15, 49
floods 5, 14-15, 30, 48, 51, 56
fog 35
forest fires 15
fronts 32-3
frost 52-3

G
gases 20-1, 56
global warming 14, 56
greenhouse effect 56
groundwater 34
Gulf Stream 12

H
hailstones 44
heat, adaptation to 16-17
helium 20
humidity 36-7
hurricanes 30-1
hygrometers 36-7, 60

I
ice ages 56
ice caps 53, 54, 56
ice storms 53
isobars 59

L
La Niña 14-15
light 42-3
lightning 44-7

M
mackerel sky 38
measurement 58-61
  humidity 36-7
  rainfall 50-1
  temperature 8-9
  wind 28-9
meteorologists 4, 51, 58-61
meteors and meteorites 56
monsoons 41, 48, 50
mountains 11, 19, 35, 52

mudslides 31, 48, 57

N
nimbus clouds 38-9, 40
nitrogen 20
Northern Hemisphere 7, 22
northern lights 18

O
ocean currents 12, 14, 56
oceans 12, 14, 34-5
oxygen 20
ozone 18, 35
ozone layer 18, 57

P
Pacific Ocean 14
pine cones 60
plants 10, 34, 36-7, 49, 54-5
polar easterlies 33
polar fronts 33
pollution 18, 19, 35, 57
precipitation 15, 34-5, 40-1, 50-2
prevailing winds 33

R
rain 34-5, 40-1, 50-1
rain gauges 50-1, 60
rainbows 42-3
rainforests 10, 36
recording measurements 60

S
savannas 10-11
seasons 7, 12
seaweed 61
sleet 52
smog 35
snow 4, 52
solar power 7
Southern Hemisphere 7, 22
southern lights 18
static electricity 46-7
Stevenson screen 9
storms
  thunder 26, 40, 44
  tropical 5, 30-1
stratosphere 18
stratus clouds 38-9

sun
  heat source 6, 34, 56, 57
  protection from 4, 12, 16-17
sunsets 19
sunshine, measurement 59

T
temperature
  changes 12-13, 56-7
  measurement 8-9
thermometers 8-9, 36, 60
thunderstorms 26, 40, 44
tidal waves 30-1
tornadoes 5, 26-7
trade winds 14, 22, 33
transpiration 34, 37
tropical climates 10
tropical storms 5, 30-1
tundra 10, 11, 54-5
twisters 5, 26-7
typhoons 30-1

U
umbrellas 50

V
volcanoes 57

W
warm fronts 32
warm temperate climates 10-11
water cycle 34-5
water vapour 34-5, 36-7, 38, 40-1, 52-3
waterspouts 26-7
weather balloons 58
weather buoys 59
weather forecasts 58-61
weather maps 60
weather satellites 58
weather stations 51, 60-1
weather vanes 28-9, 60
westerlies 33
whirlwinds 26-7
wind 22-3, 26-31, 33, 49
wind belts 22, 33, 56
wind power 23
wind-chill 8

DATE DUE